KILLER CATS

TIGERS

By Elizabeth Whyte

Gareth Stevens
Publishing

Please visit our website, www.garethstevens.com. For a free color catalog of all our high-quality books, call toll free 1-800-542-2595 or fax 1-877-542-2596.

Library of Congress Cataloging-in-Publication Data

Whyte, Elizabeth.
Tigers / Elizabeth Whyte.
    p. cm. — (Killer cats)
Includes index.
ISBN 978-1-4339-7016-0 (pbk.)
ISBN 978-1-4339-7017-7 (6-pack)
ISBN 978-1-4339-7015-3 (library binding)
1. Tiger—Juvenile literature. I. Title.
QL737.C23W536 2012
599.756—dc23

2011044903

First Edition

Published in 2013 by
Gareth Stevens Publishing
111 East 14th Street, Suite 349
New York, NY 10003

Designer: Daniel Hosek
Editor: Therese Shea

Photo credits: Cover, p. 1 Tier Und Naturfotografie J & C Sohns/Photographer's Choice/Getty Images; all backgrounds, pp. 5, 7, 9, 11, 20 Shutterstock.com; p. 13 Brendon Thorne/Getty Images; p. 15 Image Source/Getty Images; p. 17 Alexander Joe/AFP/Getty Images; p. 19 Justin Sullivan/Getty Images.

Printed in the United States of America

CPSIA compliance information: Batch #CS12GS: For further information contact Gareth Stevens, New York, New York at 1-800-542-2595.

Contents

Boldface words appear in the glossary.

Dangerous and Endangered

Tigers are the largest cats in the world. They're also one of the most feared! Tigers are skilled hunters, combining **stealth**, power, and speed to bring down their **prey**. It was once a sign of great bravery to kill this wild cat.

These days, tigers have more cause to fear people than people have to fear them. They've been hunted to such small numbers that they're now **endangered**. Though they once lived in many places, wild tigers can only be found in Asia today.

THAT'S WILD!

No two tigers have the exact same markings. Most have more than 100 stripes!

Not all tigers have orange, white, and black coloring. Some are black and tan or white and tan, and a few are even all white.

Where They Live

Tigers can live in many kinds of places, including forests, swamps, and grasslands. They like shade, and they need to be near water. In fact, many tigers love to swim.

Of course, tigers need to live in places with lots of food, too! Tigers are meat eaters, or carnivores. They eat small animals such as monkeys, turtles, frogs, and wild pigs. They also eat large animals such as deer and baby elephants. Tigers like to live and hunt alone in their own **territory**.

THAT'S WILD!

All white tigers are **related** to a white tiger that was caught in 1951. White tigers have blue eyes.

Male tigers may have longer fur around their face than females.

Clawed Killers

Tigers are deadly night hunters. Their markings help them blend in with their territory, whether they're in tall grass or a shadowy forest. Tigers have excellent eyesight and hearing. When they spot their prey, they silently follow it for as long as half an hour.

Finally, the tiger races toward the animal and uses its claws to pull the beast down. A tiger grabs large prey by the neck with its long teeth, squeezing until the animal can't breathe.

THAT'S WILD!

Like house cats, tigers draw in their claws when they aren't using them. This keeps them very sharp.

Though tigers hunt alone, they may share their kill with other tigers.

Leftovers

Tigers have a very rough tongue, almost like sandpaper! They use their tongue to clean every last bit of meat off an animal's bones. A tiger usually eats about 12 pounds (5 kg) of meat during a meal, but it can eat five times that amount.

If a tiger doesn't eat the whole animal, it may drag its prey somewhere else and hide it under leaves and dirt. Then the tiger can come back to eat when it's hungry again.

THAT'S WILD!

A tiger can drag an animal heavier than itself for more than 1/4 mile (402 m).

Tigers love water. They may chase prey into water to catch it more easily.

Tiger Cubs

Male and female tigers may share some land in their territories. Though they usually like to be alone, they come together to **mate**. A female tiger may have one to six cubs at one time.

Mother tigers raise their cubs alone. Cubs stay in the den for 6 months. Then they start to follow their mother on hunts. They may kill their first animal by the time they're 1 year old. Mother tigers guard their cubs from other wild animals that may eat them—including other tigers!

THAT'S WILD!

Tigers "talk" to each other through roars and by rubbing heads.

Tiger cubs like to play, much like kittens.

13

Growing Up

Tiger cubs stay with their mother for about 2 years. During that time, the mother provides meat for her cubs. However, she can usually only find enough food for two or three cubs. If she has more cubs, some may die from lack of food.

After 2 years, young female tigers may pick a territory near their mother. Males often go farther. Tigers live up to 20 years in the wild.

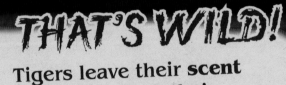

THAT'S WILD!

Tigers leave their **scent** behind to mark their territory. They also scratch trees.

Mother tigers may give birth to tigers with different colored coats from their own.

Kinds of Tigers

Only six kinds of tigers remain today: Bengal, Siberian, Indochinese, Malayan, Sumatran, and South China. Three other kinds of tigers have died off in the last 80 years. The most numerous in the wild is the Bengal, with about 1,800.

The largest tigers, Siberians, may be more than 10 feet (3 m) long and weigh as much as 650 pounds (295 kg). The smallest tigers, Sumatrans, are about 8 feet (2.4 m) long and weigh about 220 pounds (100 kg).

South China tigers haven't been spotted in the wild in 25 years, but some live in zoos.

Disappearing Tigers

Years of people hunting tigers and taking away their land have shrunk the big cat's numbers. Fewer than 3,200 tigers live in the wild today.

Despite laws, hunters still kill tigers. There's a demand for tiger parts in many areas of the world. Tigers are used for **medicine** in China. Tiger skin is used for clothing and other items. Tiger teeth and claws are even thought to be good luck by some. More must be done before teeth and claws are all that's left of these beautiful animals.

People have built homes and farms in tiger territory. This leaves tigers less land and less prey to hunt.

19

Hope for Tigers

It's not all bad news for tigers. There are many countries and wildlife groups working to help them. Some groups help track tigers in the wild. Others fight illegal hunting and selling of tiger parts. Still others work to guard the **nature reserves** that have been set up for tigers. Scientists are working to double the number of tigers over the next 10 years.

Learning more about these animals and respecting their place in nature are just a couple of ways that you can help!

THREE BIG CATS

Tigers
- striped coat
- bury prey
- largest cat

Cheetahs
- spotted coat
- claws always out
- hunt during the day

Lions
- live in groups
- solid coat
- males grow manes

Tigers ∩ Cheetahs:
- endangered
- usually live alone
- live in many kinds of places

Tigers ∩ Lions:
- hunt at night
- draw claws into paws
- like to swim

Center (all three):
- carnivores
- run fast for short distances
- good eyesight

Cheetahs ∩ Lions:
- hunts are often unsuccessful
- can go several days without water
- live in Africa

21

Glossary

endangered: in danger of dying out

mate: to come together to make babies

medicine: a drug used to treat an illness

nature reserve: a safe area for endangered animals

prey: an animal that is hunted by other animals for food

related: in the same family

scent: a smell

stealth: the act of doing something quietly and secretly

territory: an area of land that an animal lives in and guards

For More Information

BOOKS

Jenkins, Martin. *Can We Save the Tiger?* Somerville, MA: Candlewick Press, 2011.

Spilsbury, Louise. *Bengal Tiger*. Chicago, IL: Heinemann Library, 2006.

WEBSITES

Mammals: Tiger
www.sandiegozoo.org/animalbytes/t-tiger.html
Learn more about each subspecies of tiger.

Tiger
www.worldwildlife.org/species/finder/tigers/
Read what the World Wildlife Fund is doing to help tigers.

Tigers
kids.nationalgeographic.com/kids/animals/creaturefeature/tiger/
Read fun facts about tigers, and see a video of a tiger taking a bath.

Index